An Integrated Approach to
Reading and Language Arts

PLACEMENT ASSESSMENT TEACHER'S MANUAL

GRADES 1 – 6

SILVER BURDETT GINN

Needham, MA   Parsippany, NJ
Atlanta, GA   Deerfield, IL   Irving, TX   Santa Clara, CA

Silver Burdett Ginn
A Division of Simon & Schuster
160 Gould Street
Needham Heights, MA 02194

ISBN: 0-663-59587-8   3 4 5 6 7 8 9 10 CO 01 00 99 98 97 96

ACKNOWLEDGMENTS

COVER: *Design:* Dinardo Design; *Illustration:* Ashley Van Etten.

Traditionally, placement tests and informal reading inventories have been used to assist teachers in selecting an appropriate instructional level for each child in the classroom. This practice evolved from a belief that children's individual needs would best be met by changing the level of difficulty of the material. It typically leads to the formation of two or more reading groups to which children are assigned for instruction. Teachers who use ability grouping may find this use of the *Literature Works* Placement Assessment most helpful.

Teachers who adopt flexible grouping typically place each child in a grade-appropriate text. Some children, however, may require additional support so that they will experience success. In classrooms where this organizational model is being implemented, performance on the *Literature Works* Placement Assessment may be used to help teachers select appropriate instructional strategies, thereby promoting a positive reading experience for each child.

The *Literature Works* Informal Reading Inventory (IRI) is an additional component that can be used in conjunction with the Placement Assessment. Designed to be administered individually, the IRI has the student read a short passage silently and orally and then answer comprehension questions. Suggestions for effectively using the IRI with the Placement Assessment can be found in this manual.

About the Placement Assessment

The *Literature Works* Placement Assessment consists of two reading passages per grade level that are correlated to the level of difficulty of the student anthologies. For grade 1, both of the passages are fiction. For grade 2 and above, there is one fiction and one nonfiction passage per grade level.

Following each passage are multiple-choice reading questions, which assess literal, inferential, and general comprehension abilities. For grades 1–3 there are a total of ten multiple-choice questions per grade. For grades 4 and above, there are fifteen multiple-choice questions per grade. For all grades, there is one optional free-response writing question that provides an indication of how a student's general writing ability compares with that of others in the class.

Administering the Placement Assessment

Specific directions for administering the tests for grades 1–2 can be found on page T7. All directions in grades 1–2 should be read to the students. Specific directions for administering the tests for grades 3–6 are not necessary. For those grades, you may want to read the directions in the test booklets aloud with students to ensure understanding. Then instruct students to complete the test. For all grades, you may determine that going through a sample passage and set of questions before the test is beneficial to students. For example, you could write a sample question on the chalkboard, along with three or four possible answers, and then demonstrate the process.

The Placement Assessment should be administered as closely as possible to the start of instruction. It is designed to be given to small groups of students, but it can also be administered individually.

Many factors contribute to a student's performance on a test, including the student's reaction to the test itself, the testing situation, and the physical environment in which the test is given. Therefore, establish an atmosphere conducive to good testing. Try to avoid distractions during testing, and seat students so they will work independently. Allow ample time for all students to complete the test to the best of their ability. To reduce possible anxiety, give your students a clear explanation of the purpose of the test.

While administering the test, check to see that students understand all directions, are working on the correct test item, and are marking their responses appropriately. Plan testing sessions to suit your classroom situation. Because students are given two grade levels of the Placement Assessment to complete, it is recommended that you administer both grade levels during the same session. However, if your students become fatigued, stop testing and resume after the students are rested.

How to Determine Placement

Based on the information you have available, determine the last completed grade level and the expected grade level of the student. For example, if a student enters your fifth-grade classroom in September and records indicate that the student was reading at grade level last year, then the student's last completed grade would be grade 4. The student's expected grade level would be grade 5. Use the chart on page T4 to help determine which two tests to administer.

♦ **For a student who scores 60% or *below* on the first Placement Assessment, do the following:**

1. Administer the IRI at the same grade level.

2. If the IRI score is unsatisfactory, you can, depending upon your teaching strategy and the student's available records, place the student either in the last completed grade level or in his or her expected grade level and employ one of the alternate teaching strategies on page T6.

2. If a passing score is achieved on the IRI, it is recommended that you place the student at the expected grade level and administer extra help where needed.

♦ **For a student who scores *above* 60% on the first Placement Assessment, do the following:**

1. Look at the result of the second Placement Assessment administered.

2. If the student scores *60% or below,* it is recommended that you place the student at his or her expected grade level. Typically, most students will fall into this category. If you feel that additional testing is necessary, you may wish to administer the IRI at the expected grade level before placing.

2. If the student scores *above 60%,* you can, depending upon your teaching strategy, place the student either in the next higher grade level, or in his or her expected grade level and provide enrichment opportunities for the student. It is not recommended that a student be placed more than one grade level above his or her expected grade level.

Last completed grade level	Placement Assessments to administer	60% or below on 1st test, place at	60% or below on 2nd test, place at	Above 60% on 2nd test, place at
1/3	1/3, 1/4	•	1/4	2/1*
1/4	1/4, 2/1	•	2/1	2/2*
2/1	2/1, 2/2	•	2/2	3/1*
2/2	2/2, 3/1	•	3/1	3/2*
3/1	3/1, 3/2	•	3/2	4*
3/2	3/2, 4	•	4	5*
4	4, 5	•	5	6*
5	5, 6	•	6	*

• = Administer the IRI at the same grade level and refer to available student records before placing.

* = Another option: place student in expected grade level and provide enrichment opportunities.

An Example

Assume that Donny is a new student in your fourth-grade glass. If Donny's last completed grade level was 3/2, you would give him the 3/2 and 4 Placement Assessments. If he scores 60% or below on the 3/2 test, you would also administer the IRI at the 3/2 grade level. Depending on his IRI results, available student records, and your teaching strategy, Donny could either be placed at 3/2 (ability-grouped class) or at his expected grade level (4) and be given additional help (flexibly grouped class).

If Donny's score on his expected grade level test (4) is 60% or below, he should be placed at that grade (4). If his score is above 60%, you could either place Donny in the next grade level (5) and monitor his progress carefully (ability-grouped class), or place him in grade 4 and provide him with enrichment opportunities (flexibly grouped class).

Scoring and Recording the Multiple-Choice Questions

It is important to remember that the 60% score does not represent a rigid "pass/fail" mark; rather it suggests a standard of performance to be used as a criterion in making decisions about a student's placement. In addition to assessing specific skills, evaluating each student's overall performance is important. Your professional judgment, using all relevant information, including but not limited to test scores, should be the final basis for making placement decisions.

Use the following process to score and record student responses:

▶ **Determine Assessment Scores**
Using the Answer Keys found on pages T8–T9, calculate and add the number of correct responses to determine the test score.

▶ **Indicate Scores on the Student Record Form**
Write the grade levels of the two tests taken by the student in the space provided on the Student Record Form next to the appropriate test (Assessment 1 and Assessment 2). Enter the total number of items in each test and the Assessment Scores achieved by the student. Use the appropriate conversion chart to determine the percent correct, and enter it in the space provided.

▶ **Complete the Student Record Form**
If applicable, fill in the scores on the writing question and IRI for each grade level. Indicate any additional comments you might have about the student, indicating if he or she is going to require special help, additional reading material, and so on.

▶ **Complete the Class Profile**
The Class Profile is designed to help you evaluate results for individuals and groups, as well as to serve as a log to indicate those students who have gone through the placement procedure.

Using the Optional Free-Response Writing Question

There is one free-response writing question at the end of every grade level assessment. Although the student is given two grade levels of the Placement Assessment, only one writing question should be used. For scoring consistency and convenience, it is recommended that the writing question from the first test administered (the student's last completed grade) be assigned. However, you may prefer to have the student choose which question he or she would like to answer. Allow students at least twenty additional minutes to complete the writing question. Have additional paper available if students need more space than the one sheet provided.

Because the writing question in every grade level is designed to be scored holistically, the inclusion of it is optional. If you decide to use it as part of the Placement Assessment, you may wish to discuss its purpose with your students.

Scoring the Writing Question

Holistic scoring is based on the premise that writing is an integrated process that needs to be evaluated as a whole rather than by separately considering each of its parts. The total effect of a piece of writing may, in fact, differ from the sum of its parts. Holistic scoring takes into account all the major composition components of fine writing: organization, coherence, word choice, syntax, and expression of ideas. Mechanics such as spelling and punctuation are not considered unless they interfere with communicating what the writer wants to say.

Holistic scoring is a reliable method of evaluating a student's overall writing without having to stop and mark corrections, comments, and revisions. Although a holistic score does not give information about separate writing skills, it does give an overall impression of an individual's general writing ability. Just as a student's reading ability is an indicator of his or her writing ability, so is a student's writing ability an indicator of his or her reading ability.

The holistic scoring range for the writing question is from 4 to unscorable. See the Holistic Writing Evaluation Guides on pages T10–T11 for further description of the score classifications. There is one guide for grades 1–2 and another guide for grades 3–6. The numerical score should be entered on the Class Profile and Student Record Form. In addition, a descriptor should be entered on the Student Record Form, a brief statement that describes what qualities characterize a paper rated 1, a paper rated 2, and so on.

Placement Follow-up

After a period of one or two weeks in a grade level, each student's progress should be evaluated to assure proper placement. If the student is able to complete work accurately and much faster than others at the same level, additional material, such as trade books, can be assigned as enrichment.

However, if the student finds the work more difficult than do others at the same instructional level, or if the student cannot accurately complete the written work, you may want to implement one or more of the alternate teaching strategies listed below. These strategies will be particularly helpful for teachers with a flexibly grouped classroom.

Alternate Teaching Strategies

If students experience difficulty on the Placement Assessment, it may be helpful to implement instructional practices in the classroom that will familiarize students with language, vocabulary, and concepts of the student anthologies. The following recommendations provide some examples:

♦ Before reading a selection, help students to gain fluency with essential vocabulary by providing additional opportunities to read and write new words in meaningful contexts. They might use the vocabulary to formulate questions about the selection, to compose predictions, and so on.

♦ Read the selection aloud, in whole or in part, before asking students to read silently.

♦ Provide students with an oral summary of the selection, enabling them to create a framework about what they will read.

♦ Assign a partner to assist students with difficult words. Then encourage students to skim the selection before reading and to ask their partner to help them with unknown words.

PLACEMENT ASSESSMENT

SILVER BURDETT GINN

Silver Burdett Ginn
A Division of Simon & Schuster
160 Gould Street
Needham Heights, MA 02194

1997 Printing.
© 1996 Silver Burdett Ginn Inc.

ISBN: 0-663-60013-8   3 4 5 6 7 8 9 10 CO 01 00 99 98 97 96

ACKNOWLEDGMENTS

COVER: Design: Dinardo Design; *Illustration:* Ashley Van Etten.

Read each story. Then fill in the circle in front of the best answer to each question.

Where Is Koko?

Anna and her dog, Koko, were best friends. When Anna went out for a walk, Koko went with her. When Anna went to bed, Koko did too. But one day, Anna could not find Koko.

First Anna looked in her room. But Koko was not there.

Next, Anna went out to the yard. But Koko was not there.

At last Anna found Koko in the barn. She was resting next to four puppies. Koko was a mother!

Name _____

1. What might happen next in the story?

   Ⓐ Koko will find a new friend.

   Ⓑ Koko will take care of her puppies.

   Ⓒ Koko will go for a walk.

2. How did Anna most likely feel when she couldn't find Koko?

   Ⓐ happy

   Ⓑ sleepy

   Ⓒ upset

3. Why didn't Koko come when Anna called her?

   Ⓐ She was with her puppies.

   Ⓑ She was lost.

   Ⓒ She was out on a walk.

Grade 1/3 Placement Assessment

Name _____

4. What did Anna do **last** in the story?

  Ⓐ Anna went out to the yard.

  Ⓑ Anna found Koko in the barn.

  Ⓒ Anna looked in her room.

5. What **could not** happen in real life?

Bert's Surprise

Bert the mouse wanted to surprise his friends. "I will bake some muffins," Bert said. "I will give them to my friends."

First, Bert got lots of nuts. He made six muffins. They looked very fine.

Next, Bert packed the muffins and went to find his friends. He was sure they would like the surprise he made for them.

At last, Bert found his friends. He showed them the muffins. "Why, Bert!" they said. "What a nice surprise!"

Name _____

6. What will Bert and his friends most likely do next?

 Ⓐ They will eat the muffins.

 Ⓑ They will take a nap.

 Ⓒ They will get more nuts.

7. What is this story mostly about?

 Ⓐ Bert looked for his friends.

 Ⓑ Bert made a surprise for his friends.

 Ⓒ Bert got lots of nuts.

8. What happened **first** in the story?

 Ⓐ Bert showed his friends the muffins.

 Ⓑ Bert went to find his friends.

 Ⓒ Bert got lots of nuts.

9. What did Bert do **last** in the story?

Ⓐ Bert made six muffins.

Ⓑ Bert found his friends and showed them the muffins.

Ⓒ Bert packed the muffins.

10. What **could** happen in real life?

Ⓐ Ⓑ Ⓒ

Grade 1/3 Placement Assessment

Name _____

11. Bert the mouse made a wonderful surprise for his
     friends. Write about a nice surprise you would like to
     make for your friends. What is it? How would you
     make it?

     _____

     _____

     _____

     _____

     _____

     _____

     _____

     _____

     _____

Read each story. Then fill in the circle in front of the best answer to each question.

Sharing the Shade

It was a hot, sunny day. All the animals wanted to get under the tree to be in the shade. But the big hippo was already under the tree.

"Get out of the way!" growled the bear. But the hippo did not move.

"Move over!" snarled the fox. But the hippo did not move at all.

Then the rabbit spoke to the hippo in a kind way. "Hello, Hippo," said the rabbit. "Would you please move over just a bit? We are all very hot, and we would like to share the shade of this tree."

"Why, sure!" said the hippo. And he moved over so that all the animals could sit under the tree.

Grade 1/4 Placement Assessment

Name _____

1. Why did the animals want to get under the tree?

   Ⓐ to be in the shade

   Ⓑ to hide from the fox

   Ⓒ to talk to the hippo

2. Who talked to the hippo first?

   Ⓐ the rabbit

   Ⓑ the fox

   Ⓒ the bear

3. The bear and the fox were _____ to the hippo.

   Ⓐ silly

   Ⓑ good

   Ⓒ mean

Name _____

4. Why did the hippo move over at the end?

   Ⓐ The bear growled in a mean way.

   Ⓑ The rabbit asked in a kind way.

   Ⓒ The fox tricked him.

5. What time of year did this story most likely take place?

   Ⓐ fall

   Ⓑ summer

   Ⓒ winter

The Big Game

Today was the day of the big game. Lots of people had come to see it.

It was Kim's turn to bat. Her legs shook as she waited for the pitch. She took a big swing. "Strike one!" yelled the coach.

Kim gulped as she waited for the next pitch. She took another swing. "Strike two!" yelled the coach.

Kim got ready for the last pitch. She could hear everyone cheering. "Don't worry," she heard someone say. "Just do your best." Kim knew it was her friend Meg.

Kim thought of Meg's words. She watched the ball and took a big swing. WHACK! The ball went flying out into the field. Everyone cheered for Kim to run. Kim dashed to first base as fast as she could. "Nice hit!" yelled the coach.

6. How did Kim feel at the beginning of the story?

   Ⓐ scared

   Ⓑ sorry

   Ⓒ happy

7. How many times did Kim miss the ball?

   Ⓐ one time

   Ⓑ two times

   Ⓒ three times

8. Why did everyone cheer for Kim to run?

   Ⓐ Her friend was chasing her.

   Ⓑ She had to get to first base.

   Ⓒ She had missed the ball.

Name _____

9. What kind of friend is Meg?

   Ⓐ greedy

   Ⓑ helpful

   Ⓒ lazy

10. How did Kim feel at the end of the story?

   Ⓐ happy

   Ⓑ scared

   Ⓒ mad

Name _____

11. Meg's words helped Kim to hit the ball. Write about a time when someone helped you do something. What did they say or do to help you?

_____

_____

_____

_____

_____

_____

_____

_____

_____

Read each story. Then fill in the circle in front of the best answer to each question.

A Trip for a Dragon

One day a dragon came to live in a cave near the king's castle. People were afraid of the dragon.

The king said to his footman, "Get rid of that dragon!" The footman went to the dragon's cave. Soon the footman was back. "The dragon won't leave," he said. "He likes his cave and wants to stay."

Then the king asked the prince to get rid of the dragon. The prince ran to the cave. Soon he was back. "My plan didn't work AT ALL!" he said.

The princess said, "Don't worry. I'll get rid of the dragon, Father." She took a book and went out the door. Soon she was back. "Come look, Father," she said.

The king went to the window. He saw the dragon flying away. "The dragon is leaving!" said the king. "How did you do it?"

The princess said, "I gave the dragon a book to read."

"What book?" asked the king.

The princess smiled. "It is called *Fun Trips to Faraway Places*," she said.

Name _____

1. Why did the king want to get rid of the dragon?

   Ⓐ People were afraid of the dragon.

   Ⓑ The dragon ate all of the king's food.

   Ⓒ The dragon lived in the king's castle.

2. Why did the dragon want to stay?

   Ⓐ He liked the king.

   Ⓑ He liked his cave.

   Ⓒ He made a big fire near the castle.

3. Why did the dragon fly away?

   Ⓐ He was angry with the king.

   Ⓑ He was scared away by the prince.

   Ⓒ He wanted to take a trip.

Name _____

4. What kind of person is the princess?

    Ⓐ smart

    Ⓑ foolish

    Ⓒ greedy

5. Which of these **could not** be real?

    Ⓐ a king in a castle

    Ⓑ a princess with a book

    Ⓒ a dragon that can read

How Do Cats Purr?

Have you ever heard a cat purr? Do you know why and how a cat purrs? Many people think that cats purr only when they are happy. This is not true. Sometimes cats will purr when they are upset, hungry, or in pain. But how do they do it? No one really knows for sure.

One idea that people have is that purring comes from the cat's throat. As a cat breathes deeply, air passes over a piece of skin in its throat. That air makes a purring sound.

Some people have a different idea. They think that the purring sound is made when a cat's blood rushes through its body.

Cats can purr for hours, just like people can snore all night long. Even kittens that are only two days old can purr. One thing everyone can agree on is that cats do purr!

Name _____

6. What is this story mostly about?

Ⓐ how to buy a cat

Ⓑ how cats purr

Ⓒ how old cats are when they purr

7. Many people think cats purr only when they are _____ .

Ⓐ happy

Ⓑ upset

Ⓒ hungry

8. What is one idea people have about how a cat purrs?

Ⓐ As a cat breathes, air passes over a piece of skin in its throat.

Ⓑ As a cat sleeps, it makes the purring sound.

Ⓒ As a cat eats, the food makes the purring sound.

9. How long can cats purr?

   Ⓐ for a few minutes

   Ⓑ for many hours

   Ⓒ for one hour

10. Cats begin purring when they are _____ .

    Ⓐ many years old

    Ⓑ one year old

    Ⓒ a few days old

Grade 2/1 Placement Assessment

Name _____

11. Many people enjoy having a pet. Do you have a pet? Tell about
     your pet. If you don't have a pet, tell about a pet that you
     might like to have.

_____

_____

_____

_____

_____

_____

_____

_____

_____

_____

Read each story. Then fill in the circle in front of the best answer to each question.

Castles

Castles are strong buildings that are hard to break into. Kings and queens had castles built to protect themselves from enemies.

Early castles were built of wood. Later, castles were made of stone. The stone castles were much bigger and stronger than the wooden ones. Their thick, stone walls were very hard to knock down or to climb over.

Castles were built so that unfriendly people could not easily get in. Some castles were built on top of high hills. The people inside could see anyone coming. Other castles were built on flat ground. These castles often had rings of water, called **moats,** around them. The only way into the castle was by crossing a bridge over the moat. The bridge was always watched. This way only friends of the king and queen could come into the castle.

Name _____

1. Why did kings and queens have castles built?

   Ⓐ so that they would have a big home

   Ⓑ so that they could live on a high hill

   Ⓒ to protect themselves from enemies

2. What is the main idea of the second paragraph?

   Ⓐ Early castles were built of wood.

   Ⓑ Castles were strong buildings.

   Ⓒ Some castles were built of stone.

3. Choose the meaning of the word **moat** as it is used in the story.

   Ⓐ a ring of water

   Ⓑ a thick stone wall

   Ⓒ a castle made of wood

4. How did people get into a castle that had a moat?

　Ⓐ by crossing a bridge

　Ⓑ by using a boat

　Ⓒ by swimming

5. Which sentence tells the main idea of the story?

　Ⓐ Castles were built of stone and wood.

　Ⓑ Many castles had moats.

　Ⓒ Castles were built to protect people.

GO ➡

A Sweet Idea

Recess was over for the second grade class of the ABC Country Day School. It was a hot day. Lindsay and Sarah came into the building and ran to get a drink of water.

"Boy, am I thirsty!" said Lindsay.

"I wish we had lemonade," said Sarah.

Lindsay said, "I have an idea! Let's have our own lemonade stand. We can make lemonade and popcorn."

First, the two girls asked their teacher, Mrs. Brown, if they could set up a lemonade stand. Mrs. Brown thought it was a wonderful idea.

Next, the girls explained their idea to the other children in the class and asked everyone to help. Lindsay and Sarah said they would bring in paper cups. Chantel said she would bring in the popcorn, and Jeff could bring in the lemonade.

At the end of the day, Lindsay and Sarah set up the lemonade stand and put up signs. Tomorrow would be a wonderful day. The children at the ABC Country Day School would have their very own lemonade stand.

6. What was the first thing Lindsay and Sarah did?

   Ⓐ They found a good book to read together.

   Ⓑ They came in and went to get a drink of water.

   Ⓒ They explained their idea to the class.

7. What did the girls do after they talked to Mrs. Brown?

   Ⓐ They explained their idea to the other children.

   Ⓑ They tried to make lemonade in a big bowl.

   Ⓒ They drank lemonade and ate popcorn.

8. Why did the girls explain their idea to the other children?

   Ⓐ They wanted the other children to help.

   Ⓑ They had seen another lemonade stand.

   Ⓒ They wanted to make a lot of friends.

Name _____

9. What was the last thing Lindsay and Sarah did?

   Ⓐ They helped sweep the floor.

   Ⓑ They set up the lemonade stand.

   Ⓒ They sang a song to the rest of the class.

10. What is this story mostly about?

   Ⓐ making lemonade and popcorn

   Ⓑ planning a lemonade stand

   Ⓒ playing outside during recess

Name _____

11. Lindsay and Sarah had a wonderful idea to make a lemonade stand. They had their classmates help them. Write about something you did with your friends. Tell what you did and how you worked together to get it done.

_____

_____

_____

_____

_____

_____

_____

_____

_____

_____

_____

_____

Read each story. Then fill in the circle in front of the best answer to each question.

Busy as a Beaver

Have you ever heard the saying "as busy as a beaver"? Well, this saying came about after people watched beavers work. The beaver is one of the hardest-working animals.

Beavers build dams because they like to live where there is a lot of water. When beavers build a dam across a small stream, the dam acts like a wall to hold back water.

Beavers do many things to build a dam. Using their sharp teeth, they chew through tree trunks. Then the beavers chew off the branches. They work together to drag the trees to the middle of the stream. They weave leafy branches between the tree trunks. The branches **block** the stream, holding back the water. To make their dam stronger, the beavers add sticks and stones. To finish the dam, they cement everything together with thick, gooey mud.

Beavers also build houses, which are called lodges. A lodge looks like a huge pile of sticks. Like a dam, a lodge is made of sticks and stones held together with mud. But unlike a dam, a lodge is hollow in the middle so that beavers can live inside it. Beavers need a dry place to sleep, so they build the hollow space in the lodge above the water.

Beavers often work all night, building and mending their dams and lodges. It can be quite a sight to see them at work by the moonlight. Beavers certainly lead busy lives!

1. What is the main idea of this passage?

   Ⓐ A lodge looks like a huge pile of sticks.

   Ⓑ Beavers work very hard.

   Ⓒ Dams hold back water.

   Ⓓ Beavers use mud to hold their lodges together.

2. Choose the meaning of the <u>underlined</u> word as it is used in this sentence.

   The branches **block** the stream, holding back the water.

   Ⓐ a building toy

   Ⓑ a city street

   Ⓒ make

   Ⓓ stop

3. A beaver lodge is different from a beaver dam in that the lodge is _____ .

   Ⓐ hollow in the middle

   Ⓑ made of sticks and stones

   Ⓒ held together by mud

   Ⓓ built by beavers

Grade 3/1 Placement Assessment

Name _____

4. Why is the hollow part of a lodge built above the water?

   Ⓐ It is the only place beavers can store food.

   Ⓑ It is a dry place for the beavers to sleep.

   Ⓒ Other beavers will not live there.

   Ⓓ Beavers live only in the water.

5. After watching beavers work, why did people probably use the saying "as busy as a beaver"?

   Ⓐ Beavers need a dry place to sleep.

   Ⓑ Beavers work together to drag trees across streams.

   Ⓒ The beaver is one of the hardest-working animals.

   Ⓓ The beaver is a cute and fluffy animal.

A Song for Grandpa

"Practice, practice, practice," Peter thought to himself. "I don't want to practice today. It's Saturday morning, and I want to go outside and play soccer." When his dad told him that he should practice, Peter was unhappy.

Dad reminded Peter, "Grandpa's birthday is this Monday." Peter really wanted to do a good job when he played at Grandpa's party. Peter got out his violin and practiced for nearly an hour. Later that day, he found the time to play soccer, too.

On Monday, when Peter got home from school, he helped his mother put the icing and candles on the cake. Just as it started to get dark, cars began to pull up outside the house. Peter ran out to welcome his grandparents, aunts, uncles, and cousins.

After the family ate dinner, Peter's mom went into the kitchen. Peter ran to his room and carefully tuned his violin. His heart beat hard, and his hands shook a little.

When Peter walked into the room, everyone stopped talking. Suddenly all eyes were upon him. The lights went out, and his mom walked in from the kitchen holding the birthday cake.

Peter lifted his bow and began to play the song he had practiced and practiced, and everyone joined in singing. At the end of the song, everyone was quiet, but only for a second. Then they all clapped and cheered. "Bravo, Peter!" shouted Grandpa. Peter took a deep breath and smiled proudly.

Name _____

6. Why did Peter decide to practice the violin on Saturday morning?

   Ⓐ He had nothing better to do.

   Ⓑ He wanted to play well at the party.

   Ⓒ He loved to practice the violin every day.

   Ⓓ The soccer game was over.

7. When was Grandpa's party held?

   Ⓐ after lunch on Sunday

   Ⓑ Saturday morning

   Ⓒ Monday evening

   Ⓓ Monday morning

8. How did Peter feel about having to play for his whole family?

   Ⓐ bored

   Ⓑ angry

   Ⓒ sad

   Ⓓ nervous

9. What song did Peter most likely play for his grandpa?

 Ⓐ "Mary Had a Little Lamb"

 Ⓑ "Jingle Bells"

 Ⓒ "Happy Birthday"

 Ⓓ "Twinkle, Twinkle, Little Star"

10. How did Peter's grandpa probably feel about Peter's playing?

 Ⓐ He was proud of Peter's playing.

 Ⓑ He wanted Peter to play the piano.

 Ⓒ He was bored by Peter's playing.

 Ⓓ He did not like Peter's playing.

Name _____

11. Sometimes we have to practice something so that we will be able to do it well. Write about something you have to practice. It could be a game, a dance, a song, or anything else that needs work. How do you feel when you practice?

_____

_____

_____

_____

_____

_____

_____

_____

_____

_____

_____

_____

_____

37

Read each passage. Then fill in the circle in front of the best answer to each question.

Sara's Skating Rink

It was a cold Saturday morning. Sara looked outside and saw that it had snowed again. She hoped her father would drive her to the pond so that she could use her new skates.

Sara wanted to keep warm when she went outside, so she put on tights and two pairs of socks. Then she put on a pair of warm pants, a wool shirt, and her big green sweater.

When she was ready, Sara asked, "Dad, will you please take Amy and me to the ice-skating pond today?"

"Not today," said Sara's father. "The roads are too slippery."

Sara was very unhappy. She couldn't think of anything to change her father's mind. Then he had an idea to cheer her up. "Let's make a skating rink in the backyard," her father said.

"Great idea!" said Sara. "Then I can ask Amy to come over to skate."

As soon as Sara and her father finished breakfast, they put on their winter coats and went outside. First they shoveled most of the snow from the flat part of the lawn onto the hilly part. Then they hooked up the garden hose and ran water on the part they had cleared. Next Sara and her dad cleared the snow off the driveway while they waited for the water to freeze. When the water began to freeze, they added more water.

The next morning, Sara saw that the water had become a thick layer of ice. "Thank you, Dad," she said, looking at the shimmering ice.

"Thank yourself, too," said her father. "You did a lot of the work. Now you can have Amy over."

Grade 3/2 Placement Assessment

Name _____

1. What probably happened next in the story?

    Ⓐ Sara went for a drive.

    Ⓑ Sara's father made a snowman.

    Ⓒ Sara skated on the rink with Amy.

    Ⓓ Sara played at Amy's house.

2. Sara hoped that her father would drive her to the pond
    because she _____ .

    Ⓐ had shoveled the driveway

    Ⓑ wanted to keep warm when she went outside

    Ⓒ wanted to use her new skates

    Ⓓ did not want to go to Amy's house

3. Why were the roads too slippery?

    Ⓐ Sara and her father had sprayed them with water.

    Ⓑ It had snowed again.

    Ⓒ Sara wanted to go ice-skating.

    Ⓓ All the snow had melted.

4. What did Sara and her father do first to make the skating rink?

   Ⓐ They shoveled most of the snow from the flat part of the lawn onto the hilly part.

   Ⓑ They cleared the snow off the driveway.

   Ⓒ They hooked up the garden hose.

   Ⓓ They waited for the water to freeze.

5. Sara wanted to invite Amy over so that they could _____ .

   Ⓐ play in the house together

   Ⓑ hook up the garden hose to run water

   Ⓒ have lunch together

   Ⓓ skate on the backyard rink

GO ➡

An Eye on the World

Imagine not being able to watch live pictures of the news on television. How would you know what was happening? In the 1930s and 1940s, people depended on photographs to see the news. Many of the best photographs were taken by Margaret Bourke-White.

Margaret Bourke-White began working as a photographer in 1927. Her job was to take pictures of buildings. People soon noticed something special about her work. Her pictures made people feel as if they were right there, seeing things with their own eyes. Bourke-White quickly became known as a gifted photographer.

In 1929, Henry Luce asked Bourke-White to take pictures for his magazine, *Fortune.* As a photographer for *Fortune,* Bourke-White began to travel throughout the world. Then in 1936, Luce started a magazine called *Life.* He chose Bourke-White to be one of the magazine's chief photographers. As a *Life* photographer, Bourke-White joined soldiers who were fighting in World War II, which lasted from 1939 to 1945. She was the first woman photographer to see the fighting.

After the war, Bourke-White continued to take pictures of world events. She is well known for her photographs of mothers and children in India and South Africa who didn't have enough to eat. Her pictures made people want to do something to help.

For years, Margaret Bourke-White brought important events to people through her photography. Her wonderful pictures will be remembered for a long time. For many people, Margaret Bourke-White's camera was like an eye on the world.

6. What did Margaret Bourke-White do first?

   Ⓐ She began working as a photographer in 1927.

   Ⓑ She joined the soldiers who were fighting in World War II.

   Ⓒ She took photographs of people in India and South Africa.

   Ⓓ She continued to take pictures of world events after the war.

7. Henry Luce asked Bourke-White to take pictures because she _____ .

   Ⓐ had traveled a lot

   Ⓑ watched a lot of television

   Ⓒ was a gifted photographer

   Ⓓ liked buildings

8. What was Bourke-White's special role during World War II?

   Ⓐ She took photographs in India and South Africa.

   Ⓑ She fought in several battles.

   Ⓒ She was the first woman photographer to see the fighting.

   Ⓓ She took pictures of buildings.

Name _____

9. Why was Bourke-White known for her pictures of people in India?

Ⓐ She was the first woman photographer to see fighting firsthand.

Ⓑ Her pictures made people want to do something to help.

Ⓒ Her pictures of mothers and children made people happy.

Ⓓ She traveled all over the world, taking pictures for *Life*.

10. What is this passage mostly about?

Ⓐ Henry Luce's magazines, *Fortune* and *Life*

Ⓑ world events in the 1930s and 1940s

Ⓒ Bourke-White's job as a photographer

Ⓓ Bourke-White's photographs of buildings

Name _____

11. Margaret Bourke-White was known for her pictures that showed people who didn't have enough to eat. These pictures made people want to do something to help. Write about a person who has helped others in some way. Tell what this person does that is helpful.

_____

_____

_____

_____

_____

_____

_____

_____

_____

_____

_____

_____

_____

Read each passage. Then fill in the circle in front of the best answer to each question.

Elephant Talk

Elephants are mysterious creatures. Imagine a herd of elephants calmly looking for food when, suddenly, they all stop at once. For no clear reason, the elephants raise their ears and freeze in their tracks. Or sometimes, without warning, an entire herd will break into a run. These strange actions have puzzled scientists for many years.

In the early 1980s, scientists made several discoveries that helped to solve the mysteries of elephant behavior. In one new discovery, Dr. Kathryn Payne noticed that the elephants in her zoo seemed to "talk" to each other through a concrete wall. Dr. Payne made her discovery after feeling a strange throbbing in the air, much like that made by faraway thunder.

People can hear elephants make snorting, growling, and trumpeting sounds in zoos or in the wild. But elephant "talk" is too low in **pitch** for human ears to hear. Elephants use very deep rumbles to communicate with each other.

Elephants make these rumbles with a loose piece of skin that hangs in a fold above their trunks. This loose piece of skin covers a pocket of air, much like the skin of a drum. To make a rumble, an elephant moves air quickly through its trunk, which causes the piece of skin to shake and quiver. This quivering makes the deep rumbling that only other elephants can hear.

Scientists now know that elephants send messages to each other all the time. As a result, scientists understand elephant behavior that once puzzled them. When elephants suddenly stop and raise their ears, they are probably listening to distant rumbles made by other elephants. When a herd breaks into a run, it has probably received a warning. To elephants, ears are very much like radios.

1. What is the main topic of this passage?

   Ⓐ how elephants break into a run

   Ⓑ the way elephants communicate

   Ⓒ the life of elephants in zoos

   Ⓓ the low pitch of elephant talk

2. According to the passage, what strange actions of elephants have puzzled people for many years?

   Ⓐ They make snorting, growling, and trumpeting noises.

   Ⓑ They suddenly stop, or they suddenly take flight.

   Ⓒ Groups of elephants calmly look for food.

   Ⓓ Elephants seem to prefer living in zoos.

3. What did Dr. Payne discover about elephants?

   Ⓐ They can break into a run without warning.

   Ⓑ They make barking, snorting, and growling sounds.

   Ⓒ They can "talk" to each other through a concrete wall.

   Ⓓ They look for food by using sounds.

4. The strange throbbing in the air that Dr. Payne heard was most likely _____ .

   Ⓐ elephants fighting

   Ⓑ elephants breaking into a run

   Ⓒ an approaching thunderstorm

   Ⓓ the deep rumbles elephants can make

5. Choose the meaning of the <u>underlined</u> word.

   Elephant "talk" is too low in **pitch** for human ears to hear.

   Ⓐ sticky tar

   Ⓑ to set up

   Ⓒ level of sound

   Ⓓ to throw

6. How do elephants make a rumbling sound?

   Ⓐ They move air quickly through their trunks.

   Ⓑ They stamp their feet very quickly.

   Ⓒ They raise their heads and then shake and quiver.

   Ⓓ They wave their trunks in the air.

7. What are elephants probably listening to when they suddenly stop and raise their ears?

   Ⓐ the faraway sound of thunder

   Ⓑ rumbles made by other elephants

   Ⓒ their trainer in the zoo

   Ⓓ music from distant radios

8. According to the passage, what might cause a herd of elephants to break into a run?

   Ⓐ They smell a wild animal approaching.

   Ⓑ They decide that they want to play.

   Ⓒ They hear a warning from other elephants.

   Ⓓ They are in search of food and water.

Go to next page ⫸

Tanya's Latest Idea

As Tanya picked up her books, she glanced at the chalkboard. "Don't forget! Book reports due Monday. Happy weekend!" the chalk message read.

"Oh sure. Happy weekend," she muttered as she sat down next to Gloria on the bus. Tanya usually finished her book reports in one day, but she had thought about this one since Tuesday. "For our book reports, Mrs. Evans wants us to use art to tell about the main character."

"That shouldn't be hard for you," replied Gloria. "You did that great picture of Wilbur and Charlotte when you read *Charlotte's Web.*"

"That was different," replied Tanya. "Wilbur's a pig, and Charlotte's a spider. I like drawing animals, but my new book is about a real person." Tanya showed Gloria her book. "It's just as exciting and interesting as *Charlotte's Web,* but I can't think of what to do for a book report." Tanya added, "It's called *Emmiline Pankhurst.*"

"That's a strange name," said Gloria. "Who's she?"

"She was a British woman," Tanya replied. "She led the struggle for women to have the right to vote. She gave speeches. She even made a large flag that said 'Votes for Women,' and she snuck it into a room where the British leaders were meeting. She waved the flag over their heads to remind them that women really wanted the right to vote. I could draw her speaking, but I'd like to do a statue or something different."

Gloria said, "Tanya, you always have great ideas for projects. You'll think of something."

Tanya felt better as she got off the bus. Gloria always said just the right thing. As Tanya walked home, she thought more about her report. Noticing a flapping sound, Tanya stopped in front of the town hall. Looking up, she saw two flags snapping in the wind. As Tanya stood thinking, she had a brilliant idea. She knew exactly what she would do. For her book report, she would make a flag.

9. When does this passage take place?

(A) at breakfast on Monday

(B) during art class on Monday

(C) after lunch on Saturday

(D) after school on Friday

10. How is Tanya's new book different from *Charlotte's Web?*

(A) It is more exciting and interesting.

(B) It has a better title.

(C) It is more difficult to read.

(D) It is about a real person.

11. Who was Emmiline Pankhurst?

(A) a character from the story *Charlotte's Web*

(B) a British woman who spoke for women's rights

(C) a friend of Tanya's who helped her with her book report

(D) a famous British actress

12. Why did Tanya feel better as she got off the bus?

(A) She could finally go home and write her report.

(B) She was glad that the weekend was beginning.

(C) Gloria had promised to help her write her report.

(D) Gloria had cheered her up by encouraging her.

Go to next page ▶

13. Where was Tanya when she had her idea for the book report?

   Ⓐ in front of the town hall

   Ⓑ in the British leaders' room

   Ⓒ at school

   Ⓓ on the bus

14. What helped give Tanya the idea for her book report?

   Ⓐ her drawing for *Charlotte's Web*

   Ⓑ two flags snapping in the wind

   Ⓒ a statue of Emmiline Pankhurst

   Ⓓ Gloria's book report

15. Which word best describes Tanya?

   Ⓐ lazy

   Ⓑ generous

   Ⓒ creative

   Ⓓ bored

Name _____

16. Think of a book you have read recently. What was the title? Describe the book in one or two sentences. Then write about how you could use creativity—in art, music, or dance—to add to a book report about it.

_____

_____

_____

_____

_____

_____

_____

_____

_____

_____

_____

_____

_____

_____

Read each passage. Then fill in the circle in front of the best answer to each question.

Every Dollar Tells a Story

You can learn many interesting things about a country by studying its money. The symbols, words, and pictures on a coin or bill are not simply decoration. They also express a nation's values and beliefs. Tracing the history of money in the United States shows this country's development from separate colonies into a single nation.

At first, gold and silver coins from other countries were used in the colonies. Then in 1652 the English court gave the Massachusetts colony permission to make its own coins. In 1690, Massachusetts also became the first colony to make paper money.

In 1792, after the Revolutionary War had ended, the newly formed United States began issuing coins and paper money that could be used across the country. The first **mint** was established in Philadelphia. The first coins created in this mint had pictures symbolizing the beliefs of the new nation. The ten-dollar gold coin, for example, had an eagle, the symbol of power and bravery, on one side. On the other side was Liberty, shown as a woman wearing a cap.

Later coins contained the Latin words *E Pluribus Unum*. This saying means "out of many, one." It stands for the fact that the United States is a single nation formed by joining many separate colonies. *E Pluribus Unum* is the best single expression of the American ideal.

The first picture on paper money printed in the United States was of a farm. It was displayed on a bill called a "continental," named after the Continental Congress. Farming was the source of prosperity for the new nation. In later years, though, lifelike representations of famous Americans were shown on paper money. Today there are bills and coins picturing former presidents such as Washington, Lincoln, and Kennedy. There is also the Susan B. Anthony dollar. This coin was issued in honor of a leader of the movement for women's rights.

The words, symbols, and pictures on American money serve as reminders of our history. So, the next time you're handling a dollar, inspect it closely. You'll find that every dollar tells a story!

Grade 5 Placement Assessment

1. Which sentence tells the main idea of the first paragraph?

    Ⓐ You can learn many interesting things about a country by studying its money.

    Ⓑ The symbols, words, and pictures on a coin or bill are not simply decoration.

    Ⓒ They also express a nation's values and beliefs.

    Ⓓ Tracing the history of money in the United States shows this country's development from separate colonies into a single nation.

2. What was the first money used in the colonies before the Revolutionary War?

    Ⓐ coins and paper money issued from the mint in Philadelphia

    Ⓑ gold and silver coins from other countries

    Ⓒ the Susan B. Anthony dollar coin

    Ⓓ bills and coins picturing presidents of the United States

3. Choose the meaning of the underlined word as it is used in this sentence.

    The first coins created in this **mint** had pictures symbolizing the beliefs of the new nation.

    Ⓐ a piece of sweet candy

    Ⓑ a place where coins are made

    Ⓒ a very large amount

    Ⓓ a plant used for flavoring

4. Why did the ten-dollar gold coin have symbols for power, bravery, and liberty on it?

    Ⓐ The coin was from another country.

    Ⓑ Eagles were the most common birds.

    Ⓒ They were important beliefs to the newly formed United States.

    Ⓓ The Revolutionary War had just begun.

Go to next page ▶

5. What was the first picture on paper money printed in the United States?

   (A) a farm

   (B) a famous American

   (C) the White House

   (D) the Statue of Liberty

6. Why was the Susan B. Anthony dollar coin issued?

   (A) to honor those who fought in the Revolutionary War

   (B) to honor former presidents of the United States

   (C) to honor a leader of the movement for women's rights

   (D) to honor the American ideal of "out of many, one"

7. According to the passage, the words, symbols, and pictures on American money

   _____ .

   (A) serve as decoration

   (B) show what famous people in history looked like

   (C) indicate how much each coin or bill is worth

   (D) serve as reminders of our history

8. Why does the passage encourage you to inspect a dollar bill closely?

   (A) to check if it is real

   (B) to check if it is a United States bill

   (C) to see the story it tells

   (D) to see the year it was printed

Luis and the Tense Tryout

Luis huddled next to his sister Maria and whispered, "I don't know why we bothered coming. We're just wasting our time."

"Relax," she said. "You have as much of a chance as anyone, and you're a lot better than the kids we've heard so far."

They were sitting in the Civic Opera Center, several rows from the stage. The rows in front of Luis and Maria were filled with other boys and girls. Some held violins, horns, and flutes in their laps, but most were singers like Luis.

Luis turned to Maria. "But I have never starred in a show before," he protested. "You're asking me to do the impossible."

"That's ridiculous," his sister said. "You were in the musicals *The Sound of Music, Oliver!,* and *Oklahoma!*"

"But I was always part of the chorus," Luis insisted. *"The Music Man* is totally different. In this tryout, they're looking for a **soloist,** and I've never sung alone before."

"Nobody starts out as a star. You were excellent in the chorus, and now it's time to challenge yourself," Maria said.

"I just want to go," Luis insisted. It was plain to see he could not sit still much longer.

"Do you remember when you tried out for the chorus?" Maria continued. "What did they ask you to do then?"

"They just asked me to sing 'Happy Birthday'," Luis replied.

"And what did you say to me after you sang?"

"I said they would tell me I had no future as a singer and not to waste their time again."

"And what happened?"

"They invited me to join the chorus," Luis admitted.

"So what does that tell you?" Maria continued.

Luis paused for a few seconds, then flashed a smile. "It tells me I probably have fantastic talent just waiting to be discovered. For the sake of my future fans, I guess I'd better go through with this." Then he settled back into his seat.

9. What will probably happen next in the passage?

Ⓐ Maria and Luis will see a play.

Ⓑ Luis will leave the tryout.

Ⓒ Luis will sing a song for the tryout.

Ⓓ Maria and Luis will sing together.

10. How did Luis feel at the beginning of the passage?

Ⓐ nervous

Ⓑ happy

Ⓒ surprised

Ⓓ angry

11. Why was this show different from the other shows Luis had been in?

Ⓐ He played the piano in the other shows.

Ⓑ He would sing alone in this show.

Ⓒ Maria sang with him in the other shows.

Ⓓ He would not have to sing in this show.

12. What happened when Luis tried out for the chorus in other musicals?

Ⓐ They invited him to sing in the chorus.

Ⓑ He forgot the words to the song.

Ⓒ They told him he had no future as a singer.

Ⓓ They asked him not to try out again.

13. Choose the meaning of the word **soloist** as it is used in the passage.

Ⓐ a person who performs in a group

Ⓑ a person who acts in a play

Ⓒ a person who likes to sing

Ⓓ a person who performs alone

14. How did Maria help Luis?

   (A) She played the piano while he sang.

   (B) She helped him practice his songs.

   (C) She encouraged him during the tryout.

   (D) She took Luis home.

15. What is this passage mostly about?

   (A) Boys and girls sang or played instruments.

   (B) Luis was tense during the tryout for the show.

   (C) Luis got a part in *The Music Man*.

   (D) The tryout was over very quickly.

16. Luis decided to do something that was difficult for him. Write about something challenging that you have done. Tell how you felt after you did it.

   _____

   _____

   _____

   _____

   _____

   _____

   _____

   _____

   _____

   _____

Read each passage. Then fill in the circle in front of the best answer to each question.

Keeping the Roads Open

The regional weather forecast hadn't predicted a major storm, yet snow had been falling furiously for more than an hour. After dinner Chris went outside to shovel. He always tried to keep the driveway clear during a storm so that his mother's car would be ready to go. Mrs. Moore drove one of the town's snowplows, so a lot of people depended on her. Suddenly, as Chris paused to take a break, the lights along the street went out.

Chris took the flashlight from the glove compartment and made his way back to the house. As he entered the dark kitchen, his mother was lighting a candle. She said, "The telephone is out, too, so I can't call people at work. I think I'd better go. If the roads aren't open, the emergency crews won't be able to fix the telephone and electric lines. Could you come with me in case I need your help?"

Mrs. Moore dressed quickly and then she and Chris drove toward the maintenance yard where the town kept its trucks. Not more than a mile from their house, their car skidded off the road into a snowdrift. They weren't hurt, but the car was really stuck. Mrs. Moore placed some roadside flares near their car. Then she and Chris began shoveling out the front and back tires so that they could get on the road again. By the time they got to the maintenance yard, they were

cold and wet. They climbed into one of the trucks at the yard and Mrs. Moore contacted Mr. Marshall, another plow driver, on the truck's radio.

"I'm going down South Street," Mr. Marshall said. "Why don't you take the west side of town out to the Lesco house? You can stop when you get there. The Lescos will probably be serving hot food and cider."

"I think that's a great idea—we'll look forward to it," Mrs. Moore replied as she lowered the great, creaking plow and drove out of the yard. Snowflakes swirled toward the windshield as the plow hurled a constant wave of snow to the side of the road. After Mrs. Moore had plowed for several hours, she and Chris reached the Lesco house, which was brightly lit with candles and kerosene lanterns. Chris and his mother went inside and warmed themselves by the fire as Mrs. Lesco offered them refreshments. Soon Mr. Marshall, the electric and telephone repair crews, and some neighbors had also stopped by.

Chris was enjoying the talk and laughter in the crowded living room. He decided that even though the storm had been terrible in some ways, it had created warmth and friendliness among people who hadn't known each other very well before that night.

Grade 6 Placement Assessment

1. What will most likely happen next?

   Ⓐ Chris will shovel the Lescos' driveway.

   Ⓑ The Lescos' telephone will ring.

   Ⓒ Chris and his mother will go home.

   Ⓓ There will be an ice storm.

2. What time of day does this passage take place?

   Ⓐ late morning

   Ⓑ noon

   Ⓒ early afternoon

   Ⓓ evening

3. Why did people depend on Mrs. Moore?

   Ⓐ She taught at the local school.

   Ⓑ She drove one of the town's snowplows.

   Ⓒ She helped fix telephone and electric lines.

   Ⓓ She was very entertaining at parties.

4. Chris's mother decided to go to the maintenance yard when _____ .

   Ⓐ the heavy snow began

   Ⓑ the electricity and telephone went out

   Ⓒ Mr. Marshall called on the radio in his truck

   Ⓓ the weather report predicted snow

Go to next page ⦀⮕

5. Which word best describes Mrs. Moore?

    Ⓐ responsible

    Ⓑ humorous

    Ⓒ selfish

    Ⓓ reckless

6. Which word best describes Chris?

    Ⓐ careless

    Ⓑ discouraged

    Ⓒ adventurous

    Ⓓ timid

7. Why was it important for Mrs. Moore to plow the roads right away?

    Ⓐ so the roads would be clear for the morning commute

    Ⓑ so that people could drive around that night

    Ⓒ so the emergency crews could fix the lines

    Ⓓ so she and Chris could get to the Lescos' party

8. Chris thought one good thing about the storm was that _____ .

    Ⓐ he and his mother weren't hurt when the car went off the road

    Ⓑ his mother kept candles in the house in case the lights went out

    Ⓒ he could make some money by shoveling snow for people

    Ⓓ the storm had created warmth and friendliness among people

Go to next page ▓▓▓➡

Mysterious Stone Statues

On Easter Sunday in the year 1722, a Dutch explorer named Jacob Roggeveen landed on an island in the South Pacific. Roggeveen, the first European to arrive on the island, named it for the day of his landing. Today tourists still marvel, as Roggeveen must have done, at the huge stone statues scattered about Easter Island.

The statues, called *moai,* portray standing human figures. Most of the more than six hundred moai on the island are twenty feet (about seven meters) tall, but some are forty feet high. They may weigh as much as eighty tons.

These immense slabs of stone are roughly rectangular in shape. At first glance, each statue looks like a giant head because the huge eyes, nose, and mouth occupy most of the slab. The torso and limbs are much less noticeable.

All the statues were carved from dark volcanic rock. In some cases, huge stone cylinders, looking rather like hats, balance at the top of the statues. Though the statues were clearly designed to stand upright, many now rest on the ground, sightless eyes staring up at the sky.

Mysteries about the statues abound. When were they built, and why? Why are some of the statues broken?

Scientists have speculated about the answers to these questions. It appears that the island, which covers about sixty-three square miles, was first settled about 1,600 years ago, in the year 400. The settlers may have been Polynesians, but they might also have been American Indians. The statues may have been intended to honor ancestors, or they may have been part of religious ceremonies. Or, according to one modern theory, the islanders might simply have created the statues to overcome the boredom of living in such an isolated place.

The reason that some of the statues are broken is thought to be related to a civil war that broke out between two rival groups of islanders about 1675. The war continued for many years, and the winners may have turned the statues into casualties, toppling them to the ground.

While some questions about the statues' mysterious history have been answered, their strange presence continues to amaze visitors. Most visitors are likely to echo the words of an eighteenth-century sea captain who once visited the island and called the statues "the most wonderful matter my travels have yet brought me acquainted with."

9. What is the main idea of this passage?

    Ⓐ Easter Island was named by a Dutch explorer.

    Ⓑ The statues of Easter Island present fascinating mysteries.

    Ⓒ The settlers of Easter Island may have been either Polynesians or American Indians.

    Ⓓ War destroyed the civilization of Easter Island.

10. According to the passage, which of the following happened first?

    Ⓐ Roggeveen arrived at the island.

    Ⓑ Tourists visited the island.

    Ⓒ The moai were built.

    Ⓓ A civil war started.

11. What do the statues portray?

    Ⓐ standing human figures

    Ⓑ the first Europeans to arrive on the island

    Ⓒ the animals that live on Easter Island

    Ⓓ large Polynesian birds

12. About how tall are the moai?

    Ⓐ 3 to 6 feet

    Ⓑ 6 to 12 feet

    Ⓒ 12 to 18 feet

    Ⓓ 20 to 40 feet

13. In what way are all the statues alike?

    Ⓐ They are broken.

    Ⓑ They are the same height.

    Ⓒ They are carved from the same kind of rock.

    Ⓓ They are located on the same part of the island.

14. For what purpose do some scientists think the statues were built?

    Ⓐ to serve as shelters

    Ⓑ to honor ancestors

    Ⓒ to scare away enemies

    Ⓓ to serve as road markers

15. A suggested reason to explain why many of the statues are broken is that they _____ .

    Ⓐ fell over during volcanic eruptions

    Ⓑ were knocked over by the winning side in a civil war

    Ⓒ were originally designed to appear broken

    Ⓓ were carved from material that eventually falls apart

16. The mysteries of Easter Island remain unsolved, but some people think that the statues could have been created by visitors from outer space. Write about why you might want to visit another planet.

    _____

    _____

    _____

    _____

    _____

    _____

    _____

    _____

    _____

    _____

LITERATURE
WORKS

ISBN 0-663-60013-8

9 780663 600137

00001

SILVER BURDETT GINN

Assessments administered	Begin on page	End on page	Optional writing question on page
1/3, 1/4	3	16	9
1/4, 2/1	10	23	16
2/1, 2/2	17	30	23
2/2, 3/1	24	37	30
3/1, 3/2	31	44	37
3/2, 4	38	51	44
4, 5	45	57	51
5, 6	52	63	63

Directions for Assessment Administration for Grades 1/3–2/2

You may wish to write on the chalkboard the pages on which the tests begin and end. Then distribute the assessment booklets to the students. Say aloud:

Open your booklets to page (see above chart).

Look at the top of the page. Read the directions to yourself as I read them aloud: "Read each story. Fill in the circle in front of the best answer to each question." Are there any questions?

Pause and answer any questions. Then continue:

There are two stories in this test. You will read each story. Then fill in the circle in front of the best answer to each question.

If you plan to have the students complete the writing question, continue by saying:

For question number 11, you will write your answer on the lines. I will give you paper if you need more space to write your answer.

If you do not plan to have the students complete the writing question, say instead:

Do not answer the question on page (see above chart). **When you come to this page, skip it and continue on the next page.**

Finish by saying:

Put down your pencil when you come to the bottom of page (see above chart). **You may begin.**

Grade 1/3	Grade 1/4	Grade 2/1
1. B	1. A	1. A
2. C	2. C	2. B
3. A	3. C	3. C
4. B	4. B	4. A
5. A	5. B	5. C
6. A	6. A	6. B
7. B	7. B	7. A
8. C	8. B	8. A
9. B	9. B	9. B
10. C	10. A	10. C

Grade 2/2	Grade 3/1	Grade 3/2
1. C	1. B	1. C
2. B	2. D	2. C
3. A	3. A	3. B
4. A	4. B	4. A
5. C	5. C	5. D
6. B	6. B	6. A
7. A	7. C	7. C
8. A	8. D	8. C
9. B	9. C	9. B
10. B	10. A	10. C

Grade 4	Grade 5	Grade 6
1. B	1. A	1. C
2. B	2. B	2. D
3. C	3. B	3. B
4. D	4. C	4. B
5. C	5. A	5. A
6. A	6. C	6. C
7. B	7. D	7. C
8. C	8. C	8. D
9. D	9. C	9. B
10. D	10. A	10. C
11. B	11. B	11. A
12. D	12. A	12. D
13. A	13. D	13. C
14. B	14. C	14. B
15. C	15. B	15. B

Score	Descriptors
4	Demonstrates clear understanding of task
	Writing is appropriate and clear
	Elaborates on main idea
	Uses varied vocabulary
3	Writing is consistent with task
	Uses elaboration although some gaps occur
	Uses good vocabulary
2	Demonstrates some awareness of task, but writing rambles and goes off topic
	Uses adequate vocabulary
1	Demonstrates little or no awareness of task
	Writing is confusing or lacks coherence
	Uses vocabulary poorly
Unscorable	Is illegible
	Does not complete assignment

Score	Descriptors
4	Demonstrates clear understanding of task
	Writing is consistent and coherent
	Elaborates on main idea
	Uses specific and original details
	Uses vocabulary appropriately and effectively
3	Writing is consistent with task
	Uses elaboration although some gaps occur
	Includes specific details or examples
	Uses varied vocabulary
2	Demonstrates some awareness of task, but uses little elaboration
	Writing rambles and goes off topic frequently
	Details are repetitious or confusing
	Uses adequate but sometimes incorrect vocabulary
1	Demonstrates little or no awareness of task
	Writing is confusing or lacks coherence
	Details are random or inappropriate
	Uses vocabulary poorly
Unscorable	Is illegible
	Does not respond to required writing task
	Does not complete assignment

Teacher _____ Date _____

School _____ Grade _____

Students:	Placement Assessment 1	Placement Assessment 2	Writing Score	IRI Results	Placement Level
1 _____	_____	_____	_____	_____	_____
2 _____	_____	_____	_____	_____	_____
3 _____	_____	_____	_____	_____	_____
4 _____	_____	_____	_____	_____	_____
5 _____	_____	_____	_____	_____	_____
6 _____	_____	_____	_____	_____	_____
7 _____	_____	_____	_____	_____	_____
8 _____	_____	_____	_____	_____	_____
9 _____	_____	_____	_____	_____	_____
10 _____	_____	_____	_____	_____	_____
11 _____	_____	_____	_____	_____	_____
12 _____	_____	_____	_____	_____	_____
13 _____	_____	_____	_____	_____	_____
14 _____	_____	_____	_____	_____	_____
15 _____	_____	_____	_____	_____	_____
16 _____	_____	_____	_____	_____	_____
17 _____	_____	_____	_____	_____	_____
18 _____	_____	_____	_____	_____	_____
19 _____	_____	_____	_____	_____	_____
20 _____	_____	_____	_____	_____	_____

Student Name _____

Date _____ Last Completed Grade Level _____

Teacher _____ School _____ Grade _____

	Total Number of Items	Assessment Score	Percent Correct	Writing Score (optional)	IRI Results (optional)
Assessment 1 Grade Level ____ (Last completed)			%		
Assessment 2 Grade Level ____ (Expected)			%		

Conversion Charts

For 10 Question Assessment (Grades 1/3–2/2)

Number of Items Correct		1	2	3	4	5	6	7	8	9	10
Percent Correct		10%	20%	30%	40%	50%	60%	70%	80%	90%	100%

For 15 Question Assessment (Grades 3/1–6)

Number of Items Correct	1	2	3	4	5	6	7	8	9	10	11	12	13	14	15
Percent Correct (rounded)	7%	13%	20%	27%	33%	40%	47%	53%	60%	67%	73%	80%	87%	93%	100%

▶ **Observations:** ....
....
....

▶ **Recommendations:** ....
....
....

T13